AF433582

Day & Night: Contemplative Prayer Guide and Journal
by Catherine Weiskopf
copyright 2020 Catherine Weiskopf

ISBN: 9798565357554

Cover art by Catherine Weiskopf

DAY & NIGHT

Contemplative Prayer Guide
and Journal

BY CATHERINE WEISKOPF

Contemplative Prayer is a life-giving and depth-building form of prayer that offers more freedom in how we communicate with God. While both traditional memorized prayer and prayers of petition are wonderful, we can also pray by using our imagination, welcoming silence, wrestling with our theology, and reviewing our day. Contemplative prayer is as varied as the God we love.

With so many wonderful prayer options, developing a habit can be overwhelming. This journal, laid out with contemplative practices both day and night, can help establish this peace-producing, contemplative habit. Welcome each morning with a unique contemplative prayer and close out each evening with The Examen. After each prayer there is space to journal.

Contemplative prayer greatly increased my prayer life because it expanded my definition of prayer and my prayer options. It also infused new life into my prayer time by offering me exciting variety. In this journal you will find guidance on how to do many contemplative types of prayer including:

The Examen
Lectio Divina
Personal Lectio
Ignatian Contemplation
A Litany
Contemplative Reflection
The Breath Prayer
Centering Prayer
Guided Meditation

While all these above prayer types are introduced here, please be aware that some of them have whole books written about them. If one prayer type speaks to you, please seek out additional guidance. Also, know that it has been my experience that different prayer types have been helpful for different times in my life. So remember that just because you find one type difficult now, doesn't mean that months or years down the road it won't nourish your soul.

I hope and pray that God will use *Day & Night: Contemplative Prayer Guide and Journal* to richly bless you.

Cathy

Guidelines for Contemplative Prayer

If you have not practiced meditation or any of these contemplative prayer forms, it is important to welcome a different stance with regards to your mind and yourself in general.

A helpful meditative stance, with regards to the mind, is to observe your thoughts like an uninterested third-party. Let your thoughts come in and go out rather than actively trying to prevent yourself from thinking or getting upset when you get distracted. Below are a few techniques to help you establish distance between you and your thought.

- As thoughts come into your mind and try to engage you, imagine they are on a thought train and watch your thoughts slowly move away from you as they chug down the tracks.
- Similarly, instead of getting attached to your thoughts, imagine them on a hot-air balloon and watch them float away or drift away on the sails of a boat. See the hot-air balloon or sailboat getting smaller and less significant as it moves toward the horizon.
- Think of thoughts as rabbits or squirrels. Every thought that crosses your mind doesn't have to be chased after, like a dog on a walk. Just let the rabbits or squirrels scamper on their way.

With regards to yourself, acceptance and compassion for yourself on this journey is important. Silence, inner peace, and calmness are rare states in our modern world and the path to them is different than anything you've done before. Surrender, not striving, is the way.

While it can be easy in calmness to slip into sleep, it may be helpful to sit will doing these practices to set your intention upon remaining awake in this process.

Morning Prayer

Litany

A litany is a series of repetitive petitions often preformed in church. You can adapt this prayer form for your own personal use by creating litanies of your own. To create a litany start with one line from your favorite scripture and use that as the beginning of each new line of petition. Give yourself as much time as needed in between individual petitions to let your heart pray.

The following litany was created from Ephesians 1:18 which says, "I pray that the eyes of your heart may be enlightened in order that you may know the hope to which he has called you, the riches of his glorious inheritance in his holy people, and his incomparably great power for us who believe." (NIV)

From the above scripture our litany becomes: Open the Eyes of my heart, Lord, I want to see . . .

Please add what you want to see, experience, or love after each iteration of the litany. Continue for as long as you want. Below are a few examples.

- Open the Eyes of my heart, Lord, I want to see my enemies through your eyes.
- Open the Eyes of my heart, Lord, I want to see what you want me to see.
- Open the Eyes of my heart, Lord, I want to see your truth.
- Open the Eyes of my heart, Lord, I want to see . . .

When you are done, journal about your experience on the next page.

Evening Prayer

Dear God, thank you for your love! Help me to review my day through the eyes of your grace and notice the ways you are working on me.

As I review my day, help me to notice moments that were great blessings and moment where I recognized your presence.

____

____

____

____

____

____

____

____

____

____

____

____

____

____

____

____

____

____

____

____

____

____

Dear God, thank you and guide me tomorrow along your holy path.

Morning Prayer

Lectio Divina

Lectio Divina means divine reading in Latin. There are many ways to do Lectio Divina but they all include the following basic components:

- **Lectio**- Reading of the scripture in a slow reflective way. This reading is often done more than one time, so the chosen passage of scripture should not be too long.
- **Meditatio**- Reflecting and meditating on scripture. This stage often involves reading the scripture again.
- **Oratio** - Speaking your heart to God.
- **Contemplatio** - This word means rest. This stage is where you let go, not only of your own ideas and plans, but also of your thoughts. Simply rest in the Word of God.

These four key components can be put together in a multitude of ways. Here is one possible structure for Lectio Divina with the scripture. Feel free to adjust the time. Minutes are noted to give you an idea of possible practice.

Lectio Divina on 2 Corinthians 4:16-18

Prepare for the Reading of the Word
Take three nice slow deep breaths and feel yourself relaxing.

Lectio
Read the below scripture and notice a word or phrase that catches your attention or tugs at your heart.

Therefore we do not lose heart. Though outwardly we are wasting away, yet inwardly we are being renewed day by day. For our light and momentary troubles are achieving for us an eternal glory that far outweighs them all. So we fix our eyes not on what is seen, but on what is unseen, since what is seen is temporary, but what is unseen is eternal. (NIV)

Contemplatio (2 + min.)
Sit quietly and rest and prepare yourself to hear the word again.

Lectio
Read the scripture again and notice a word or phrase that captures your attention.

Therefore we do not lose heart. Though outwardly we are wasting away, yet inwardly we are being renewed day by day. For our light and momentary troubles are achieving for us an eternal glory that far outweighs them all. So we fix our eyes not on what is seen, but on what is unseen, since what is seen is temporary, but what is unseen is eternal.

Meditatio (5 + min.)
Spend some time meditating on your word or phrase. Allow God to speak to any situation you are going through using this scripture.

Oratio(5 + min.)
Speak your heart to God about your meditation and journal below.

____

____

____

____

____

Evening Prayer

Dear God, you say I am the light of the world. Help me to be aware of when my light shines and when it is dull.

When today did I live into my roll as the light of the world?

____

____

____

____

____

____

____

____

____

____

When today was my light dim or seemingly non existent?

____

____

____

____

____

____

____

____

____

____

Dear God, thanks for today and for your guidance in this examen. I ask for your help and direction tomorrow so that I might follow your plan for my life more closely.

Morning Prayer

Guided Meditation

Read over the following meditation slowly and allow moments of silence after each ellipsis. Refer back to this page when necessary. You can also record this meditation on your phone.

Take a few minutes and review your last week. Search for an emotion that draw your attention - an emotion you resist, one that is unpleasant, or common. Choose one emotion you would like to focus on during this morning prayer. . .

Once you have this emotion, take a few deep breaths and relax. As you continue to breath deeply, become aware of Jesus standing before you. . . Slowly become cognizant that he is holding a gift for you. . . As he hands the package to you, see the label on the gift bearing the name of the emotion you selected above. . . See how the outside of the package looks. Is it dark or light? Pretty or unattractive? Is the package heavy or light? . . .

Begin slowly opening the package as Jesus encourages you. . . Peel back the paper. Are you hesitate or excited?. . As you remove the final wrappings become aware of what is inside. . . Notice the gift of this emotion. Is this emotion showing you something about yourself or your relationships?. . . Does the inside look different from the outside? See it as clearly as you can . . . What is the invitation from this emotion? How can this emotion help you draw you closer to Jesus?

Now end this time by thanking Jesus for the gift of this emotion and asking Jesus to help you use it in the way the gift was intended.

Evening Prayer

Dear God, your love for this world gives me hope. Help me to focus today on the presence and absence of hope in my life.

When today did I feel hopeful? Were there times when I spread that hope?

____

____

____

____

____

____

____

____

____

____

When today did I let bad news or bad feelings get the best of me and spread gloom and doom instead of hope?

____

____

____

____

____

____

____

____

____

____

Dear God, thanks for today and for your guidance in this examen. I ask for your help and direction tomorrow so that I might follow your plan for my life more closely.

Morning Prayer

A Blessing Prayer

Spend the next few minutes offering blessings: first to your-self, then to a loved one, and finally to someone who may be difficult to bless. As you say the blessing, either out loud or to yourself, you can use your imagination to envision God's love surrounding them, light bathing them, or whatever is comfort-able for you.

Take a deep breath, and if you feel comfortable, close your eyes.
Start this blessing process with blessing yourself. Say the fol-lowing blessing:
May I feel joy.
May I be content.
May I know God's love and feel his peace.

Let the peace and love of God soak into you at the deepest level as you now think of a person that you love and who you would like to bless today. . . . . . . Imagine them standing be-fore you or imagine their face as you bless them.
May you feel joy
May you be content.
May you know God's love and feel his peace.

Now think of someone in your life who is harder to bless. Someone who rubs you the wrong way, or you've had an argument with, or someone who perhaps you don't believe deserves a blessing. . . . . . . Imagine their face or imagine them standing before you as you bless them.
May you feel joy.
May you be content.

May you know God's love and feel his peace.
Continue blessing people for as long as you would like and
then finish by journaling.

Evening Prayer

God, as I review my day, help me to be aware of moments when you were clearly working both on me and in my life and when I was attempting to run the other way.

When did it seem that God was most involved with me today?

____

____

____

____

____

____

____

____

____

____

____

____

____

____

____

____

____

____

____

____

____

Dear God, thanks for today and for your guidance in this examen. I ask for your help and direction tomorrow so that I might follow your plan for my life more closely.

Morning Prayer

The Breath Prayer

The name of the breath prayer perfectly describes what it is: a prayer done with the flow of your breath. It is a repetitious prayer where you breathe in as you call on Jesus and breathe out as you repeat your petition. It is also often called the Jesus prayer. Below are a few variations of this traditional prayer form.

Lord Jesus Christ, have mercy.
Lord, have mercy on me a sinner.
Lord, have mercy.

In this practice, say "Lord Jesus Christ" to yourself as you breathe in and say "have mercy" as you breathe out. Please choose which version you want to use and repeat it for 5 or 10 minutes while slowly breathing in and out. Then journal about this experience.

____

____

____

____

____

____

Evening Prayer

Dear God, it seems an impossible task to love you with all my heart. Help me be aware of my breakthrough moments of love and my moment when fear and doubt dominated.

When did I love God and others today?

____

____

____

____

____

____

____

____

____

____

When were fear and doubt my major emotions?

____

____

____

____

____

____

____

____

____

____

Dear God, thanks for today and for your guidance in this examen. I ask for your help and direction tomorrow so that I might follow your plan for my life more closely.

Morning Prayer

A Personal Breath Prayer

Design your own personal breath prayer with these simple
steps.

- Start with your favorite name for God. You can look to
  scriptures for these names but here are a few suggestions:
  Jesus, Creator, Father, God, Counselor, Prince of Peace,
  Savior, Redeemer, Emanuel, Lord, Mighty One, King,
  and Shepherd.
- Next consider what you desire or want from God today?
  If you have a specific request make it as short as possible
  and general as possible. Let general words represent your
  request.
- Put the two parts together. As you breathe in, say to
  yourself, your name for God. As you breathe out, state
  your want or desire for today.

For example: Shepherd, guide me in your ways.
                or Jesus, grant me peace.

Following the rhythm of your breath, repeat your personal
breath prayer for at least five minutes and then journal about
the experience. Please note your chosen breath prayer.

____

____

____

____

Evening Prayer

God, help me to be aware of ways in which you delighted in me today and ways in which I was not as delightful.

When did I feel most delighted about my day or when did I feel God's delight in me as part of his creation?

____

____

____

____

____

____

____

____

____

____

____

____

____

____

____

____

____

____

____

____

Dear God, thanks for today and for your guidance in this examen. I ask for your help and direction tomorrow so that I might follow your plan for my life more closely.

Morning Prayer

Ignatian Contemplation

Ignatian contemplation is a prayer form that invites you to imagine and engage in scripture to experience the love of God and the life of Jesus. If using your imagination this way feels uncomfortable and sacrilegious, remember that God designed your imagination, so begin by praying for God's guidance.

Begin by reading Luke 13:10-17 a couple of time:
Jesus was teaching in one of the synagogues, and a woman was there who had been crippled by a spirit for eighteen years. She was bent over and could not straighten up at all. When Jesus saw her, he called her forward and said to her, "Woman, you are set free from your infirmity." Then he put his hands on her, and immediately she straightened up and praised God. (NIV)

Now allow yourself to enter the scene as an observer. Pause as you read and allow yourself to engage in the scene.

Imagine the synagogue around you as you join the scene of Jesus teaching. Take a moment to feel what the room is like. . . Is it dimly lit or bright? Warm or cold? Is it packed or almost empty? On one side of the room you see and hear Jesus surrounded by a group of people listening and talking to him. See Jesus interacting with them. See his face? His posture? Hear the tone of his voice. Get a sense of Jesus being in this space. . .

Now picture the people around him. . . How many can you see? Who is present and who is not? Who is paying attention? Who seems to be more concerned with other things?

Now get closer to Jesus. As you draw closer, Jesus stops talking and looks up. You see him make eye contact with a woman across the room. He calls her over. Notice the woman's reaction to his call.

Now the woman approaches him. What does she look like? How does she move? She seems to be well known in the synagogue as people are whispering about her being this way for 18 years. As she gets closer how are the people around Jesus reacting? Are they inviting or annoyed by this intruder who has Jesus' attention? How do their reactions differ from how Jesus is reacting to her?

Does she seem worried or comfortable? Is her head up or bowed down? Jesus directs her to come closer and he takes her hand and says the words, "Woman, you are freed from your disability." What happens to her after Jesus says the words. How does she change?

As you end this prayer time, thank God for this experience and enter your time of journaling by asking yourself: What challenged you? Where did you sense God the most? What emotions were you aware of? What did you resist?

____

____

____

____

____

____

____

____

Evening Prayer

Holy God, you love my humbleness and abhor pride. Help me to lovingly look at when I experienced each today?

When was I humble today?

____

____

____

____

____

____

____

____

____

____

When did pride get in the way of my work, accepting valid criticism, enjoying a conversation, or being happy for others?

____

____

____

____

____

____

____

____

____

____

Dear God, thanks for today and for your guidance in this examen. I ask for your help and direction tomorrow so that I might follow your plan for my life more closely.

Morning Prayer

Ignatian Contemplation

In the last morning prayer you put yourself in the gospel story Luke 13:10-17 as an observer. Today imagine you are the woman who was healed. Begin once again by reading the scripture:

Jesus was teaching in one of the synagogues, and a woman was there who had been crippled by a spirit for eighteen years. She was bent over and could not straighten up at all. When Jesus saw her, he called her forward and said to her, "Woman, you are set free from your infirmity." Then he put his hands on her, and immediately she straightened up and praised God. (NIV)

Imagine the synagogue around you as you join the scene of Jesus teaching. On one side of the room you see and hear Jesus surrounded by a group of people talking to him. Become aware that you are on the other-side of the room.

As you stand there become aware of someone calling your name. You look up and see Jesus looking at you. Notice his eyes and gesture as you hear him call your name again.

Begin approaching Jesus. Are you dragging your feet or hurried? Are you nervous or excited? Hear the whispers around you as and notice how they make you feel. Notice the reaction of the people around Jesus. Do they make room for you in the group?

Hear Jesus inviting you closer. Feel his touch as he takes your hand and says the words, "Woman, you are set free from your disability."

What happens to your body and spirit after Jesus says the words. How does this change feel? How does it feel to be healed?

Take a moment and picture yourself thanking Jesus for the healing.
See your joy. . . See his joy . . .

As you enter your time of journaling ask yourself: What stood out
to you in prayer? What challenged you? Where did you sense God
the most? What emotions were you aware of? What did you resist?

____

____

____

____

____

____

____

____

____

____

____

____

Evening Prayer

God, help me be aware of the times today that I noticed and appreci-ated your majesty and Also help me to remember when I got stuck in complaining.

When today was I in awe of the world God created?

____

____

____

____

____

____

____

____

____

____

When today did I feel stuck in complaining?

Dear God, thanks for today and for your guidance in this examen. I ask for your help and direction tomorrow so that I might follow your plan for my life more closely.

Morning Prayer

Contemplative Reflection

Contemplative reflection is an unusual form of contemplative prayer that involves struggling with an issue or concept. It is sometimes described as wrestling with God.

When done on your own it involves choosing an article, quote, scripture, poem, or other religious text that is focused on a topic like love, faith, justice, or hope, for a few examples. Begin by asking God to guide your thoughts. Next, read the selected material and spend the chosen period of time contemplating the topic. For this morning's contemplative reflection read the below quote from *Addiction and Grace* by Gerald G. May, M.D. on hope:

"Because of God's continuing love, the human spirit can never be completely obliterated. No matter how oppressed we are, by other people and circumstances or by our own internal addictions, some small capacity for choice remains unvanquished. . . The bare edge of freedom is insured and preserved inside us by God, and no matter what forces oppress us from without or within, it is indestructible."

Meditate or wrestle with the topic for 10 minutes or more. End by journaling about the experience.

____

____

____

____

Evening Prayer

Holy God, help me to notice the moments in my day that were filled with compassion and also those moment when compassion was far from my heart.

When today was I compassionate to both others and myself?

____

____

____

____

____

____

____

____

____

____

When today was I impatient and uncaring both to other people's difficulties and my own?

____

____

____

____

____

____

____

____

____

____

Dear God, thanks for today and for your guidance in this examen. I ask for your help and direction tomorrow so that I might follow your plan for my life more closely.

Morning Prayer

Centering Prayer

This is a simple prayer form in terms of instructions, but not in terms of practice. Before you begin:
- Decide how long you will be doing this prayer: 20 minutes is a good amount of time but start with 10 minutes if you have never done it before.
- Choose a sacred word that you will use to bring your attention back to sitting in silence and reaffirming your intention to surrender to the mystery of God.
- Find a comfortable place where you can sit.
- Remind yourself that just like your lungs breathe, your mind thinks, so try not to be upset by your distractions. Each time your mind wanders, simply bring your attention back to your sacred word.
- This prayer type fosters knowledge of God through experience.

Begin by asking Jesus to become real to you during this time of prayer and to help you let go of any specific outcomes for the time spent.

Take a few nice slow deep breaths and say your sacred word to yourself. Then begin to quietly sit and be open to being with God. Continue to say your word whenever any distracting thoughts come into your mind. Allow this word to bring you back to inner quietness.

When your set time is over, end by thanking God for this gift of silence and presence. Finally, journal for a few minutes.

____

____

Evening Prayer

Dear God, I know you tell me that I should take refuge in you, but I often don't. Help me to be honest about the times that I take refuge in other things and people instead of running to you.

When today did I take refuge in God?

____

____

____

____

____

____

____

____

____

____

When today did I run anywhere but to Jesus when I had troubles?

____

____

____

____

____

____

____

____

____

____

Dear God, thanks for today and for your guidance in this examen. I ask for your help and direction tomorrow so that I might follow your plan for my life more closely.

Morning Prayer

Lectio Divina

Prepare for the Reading of the Word
Take three nice slow deep breaths and feel yourself relaxing.

Lectio
Read the below scripture and notice a word or phrase that catches your attention or tugs at your heart.

In the beginning was the Word, and the Word was with God, and the Word was God. He was with God in the beginning. Through him all things were made; without him nothing was made that has been made. In him was life, and that life was the light of all mankind. The light shines in the darkness, and the darkness has not overcome it. (John 1:1-5 NIV)

Contemplatio (2 + min.)
Sit quietly, rest and prepare yourself to hear the Word again.

Lectio
Read the scripture again and notice a word or phrase that captures your attention.

In the beginning was the Word, and the Word was with God, and the Word was God. He was with God in the beginning. Through him all things were made; without him nothing was made that has been made. In him was life, and that life was the light of all mankind. The light shines in the darkness, and the darkness has not overcome it.

Meditatio (5 + min.)
Spend some time meditating on your word or phrase. Allow God

to speak to any situation you are going through using this scripture.

Oratio(5 + min.)
Speak your heart to God about your meditation and then take a few minutes to journal.

____

____

____

____

____

____

____

____

____

____

____

____

Evening Prayer

Dear God, sometimes during the day I draw closer to you and sometimes I find I just want to do my day my way. Help me to be aware of these moments and their affects on both my spirit and my relationships.

When did I draw closer to God today?

____

____

____

____

____

____

____

____

____

____

____

What moments today did I move away from God in my thoughts and actions?

____

____

____

____

____

____

____

____

____

____

Dear God, thanks for today and for your guidance in this examen. I ask for your help and direction tomorrow so that I might follow your plan for my life more closely.

Morning Prayer

A Personal Lectio

Listen to Your Week

As you relax, take a couple of minutes to review the moments of your week. Allow each event and interaction to gentle move into and out of your awareness. As you continue to breath deeply, begin to focus on one occasion that seems to pull your attention and have more emotional energy.

Listen to the Moment

Now sit with this occasion or event for a couple of minutes and recreate the physical event as much as possible. Remember the sounds, colors, smells, and how it progressed. Then remember your emotions during this event. When were your emotions the strongest? How did they feel in your body? Especially notice any change in your emotions. Spend a couple of minutes contemplating this event.

Listen to God

Now allow yourself to let go of this moment. Let go of the feelings you experienced during the event and allow your mind to go as blank as possible. Release everything about this moment to God. With a blank mind invite God to give you an image, a phrase, a song, a thought or a scripture that relates to this moment. Be open to whatever comes to mind without having to understand how it relates to your moment. Trust and accept it gratefully.

Offering

Now in your mind, take the incident, and the image or phrase given by God, and place them both on an offering plate. Offer this plate with its images up to God. Give God all that was done and all that wasn't, all you regrets and all you are thankful for. Give it all back to God as you open yourself to any gifts God wants to give you through this prayer.

Thanksgiving
End with a prayer of thanksgiving for any grace, any gifts, or any struggles that you received during this prayer time. Finish with a few minutes of journal writing.

Adapted from A Personal Lectio Process from Heartpath DFW

____

____

____

____

____

____

____

____

____

____

____

Evening Prayer

Dear God, there are people, that in my opinion, have wronged me and my loved ones. Blessing them, forgiving them, is your will but I admit it is difficult to even want their lives to turn out well. Help me to let go of my grievances today and every day.

When today did I work on blessing my enemies or at least not wishing them harm? When did I want good for people who seem to not want good for me?

Who did I have trouble forgiving today? What "wrong" did I keep wanting to bring up? When I prayed who was it hard to pray for?

____

____

____

____

____

____

____

____

____

____

Dear God, thanks for today and for your guidance in this examen. I ask for your help and direction tomorrow so that I might follow your plan for my life more closely.

Morning Prayer

Guided Meditation

God instructs us to keep his words written on the tablet of our hearts, yet many times our hearts are divided. This meditation centers around Proverbs 7:1-3: "My son, keep my words and treasure up my commandments with you; keep my commandments and live; keep my teaching as the apple of your eye; bind them on your fingers; write them on the tablet of your heart." (NIV)

Read over the following meditation slowly, resting each time there are ellipsis. Refer back to these pages when necessary. You can also record this meditation on your phone.

Close your eyes and take a few nice deep breaths . . . Breathe in love and breathe out anything that is stopping you from giving and receiving love . . .

See yourself in a room . . . a relaxing peaceful room. You are waiting for someone. . . There is a light knock at the door and you get up to answer. . . Jesus has come to visit you. . . Invite him into your space.

As you sit with Him, you see Jesus' heart . . . You are aware that he also sees your heart and loves it. . . Feel the love he has for you. . . As he is loving your heart he asks you, "What is written on the tablet of your heart."

You think about what has seemed most important to you during the last month, or week, or day, or even hour. . . What has captured your focus? . . . What has occupied most of your time and attention? Talk to Jesus about these event, or emotions that are currently written on the tablet of your heart. . .

After talking with Jesus, he asks you, "Would you like for something else to be written on the tablet of your heart?". . . Spend a few minutes and consider the answer to his question. . . You answer with what you would like to be most important in your life. . .

As you sit and continue to talk to Jesus, you see and feel a change in the tablet of your heart. . . It could be words are fading. . . It could be that old words are being erased and it could be new words are being written. . . Allow yourself to enjoy the love and acceptance flowing from Jesus as the change happens. . .

As your time with this meditation comes to a close, enjoy Jesus' embrace. . . When you are ready stretch and open your eyes aware of the love you felt and the change in your heart that is beginning.

____

____

____

____

____

____

____

____

____

Evening Prayer

Dear God, help me to clearly see your many blessings and be aware of when I focus on what I don't have.

Fill the page with thanksgiving for God's blessings today. Don't forget both the small and large blessings of life.

____

____

____

____

____

____

____

____

____

____

Review your day and notice when today have you focused on what you don't have.

____

____

____

____

____

____

____

____

____

____

Dear God, thanks for today and for your guidance in this examen. I ask for your help and direction tomorrow so that I might follow your plan for my life more closely.

Morning Prayer

A Subtractive Litany

My name for this type of prayer comes from the fact that it both loses words with each iteration and is a repetitive petition.

From Ephesians 1:18 (NIV)
I pray that the eyes of your heart may be enlightened in order that you may know the hope to which he has called you. . .

Begin with the paraphrased verse below and then with each repetition lose the last word or phrase. Leave a minute of silence after each line to meditate on what calls to your heart in each repetition.

Open the eyes of my heart, Lord, I want to see you.
Open the eyes of my heart, Lord, I want to see.
Open the eyes of my heart, Lord.
Open the eyes of my heart.
Open my eyes
Open

Finish by spending a few minutes journaling about your experience.

____

____

____

____

Evening Prayer

Dear God, help me to review my day through the eyes of your grace and love and notice the ways you are working on me and nudging me in your direction.

When did I say "yes" to God's promptings and direction today?

____

____

____

____

____

____

____

____

____

____

What opportunities did I miss today to live as God desires?

____

____

____

____

____

____

____

____

____

____

Dear God, thanks for today and for your guidance in this examen. I ask for your help and direction tomorrow so that I might follow your plan for my life more closely.

Date: _________________

Morning Prayer

Ignatian Contemplation

Begin by reading Matthew 14:13-21 a couple of times to become familiar with the story.

"As evening approached, the disciples came to him and said, 'This is a remote place, and it's already getting late. Send the crowds away, so they can go to the villages and buy themselves some food.' Jesus replied, 'They do not need to go away. You give them something to eat.' 'We have here only five loaves of bread and two fish,' they answered. 'Bring them here to me,' he said. And he directed the people to sit down on the grass. Taking the five loaves and the two fish and looking up to heaven, he gave thanks and broke the loaves. Then he gave them to the disciples, and the disciples gave them to the people." (NIV)

Now allow yourself to enter the scene as either a character or an observer.

Take a few deep breaths and relax. . . Get a sense of yourself standing on a hill on a beautiful day. Notice the sky. Allow yourself to absorb the scene around you. How many people are there with you?. . . Observe Jesus talking to the disciples. How are they reacting as they discuss how to feed the people? . . . See Jesus giving them instructions. He instructs the crowd to sit down. You listen and wait.

See Jesus breaking the bread and talking to God. Notice him giving more and more food to the disciples both bread and fish. Observe the disciples giving it to the people. How do you react to this gift of food?

How does the bread taste? How does it look? How is the fish? Does it satisfy your hunger?

Notice where Jesus is as you imagine yourself eating. . . How is he interacting with the crowd. How do you feel as you finish this meal?

Thank Jesus for what he has given you as you end this time of contemplation. Then enter your time of journaling asking yourself: What stood out to you in prayer? What challenged you? Where did you sense God the most? What emotions were you aware of?

____

____

____

____

____

____

____

____

____

____

____

Evening Prayer

God, guide me in this honest examen today. Help me look at this day and everyday with appreciation and honesty.

For which moments today am I most thankful?

____

____

____

____

____

____

____

____

____

____

For which moments today am I least thankful?

____

____

____

____

____

____

____

____

____

____

____

Dear God, thanks for today and for your guidance in this examen. I ask for your help and direction tomorrow so that I might follow your plan for my life more closely.

Date: ___________________

Morning Prayer

Contemplative Reflection

Contemplative reflection is an unusual form of contemplative prayer that involves struggling with an issue or concept. It is sometimes described as wrestling with God.

When done on your own it involves choosing an article, quote, scripture, poem, or other religious text that is focused on a topic like love, faith, justice, or hope, for a few examples. Begin by asking God to guide your thoughts. Next, read the selected material and spend the chosen period of time contemplating the topic. For this morning's contemplative reflection read the below quote from Richard Rohr from *Everything Belongs* about justice.

"When we can see the image of God where we don't want to see the image of God, then we see with eyes not our own."

Meditate or wrestle with the topic for 10 minutes or more. End by journaling about the experience.

____

____

____

____

____

____

Evening Prayer

Dear God, help me to be aware of both the people who have helped me in my faith today and the people I have helped.

Where have I exercised my faith today? Where have I encouraged other people's faith?

When today have I succumb to fear? Where have I taught people the importance of listening to fear instead of faith?

____

____

____

____

____

____

____

____

____

____

Dear God, thanks for today and for your guidance in this examen. I ask for your help and direction tomorrow so that I might follow your plan for my life more closely.

Morning Prayer

A Personal Breath Prayer

Design your own personal breath prayer with these simple steps. This prayer may be prayed out loud or to yourself.

- Start with your favorite name for God. You can look to scriptures for these names but here are a few suggestions to get you started: Jesus, Creator, Father, God, Counselor, Prince of Peace, Savior, Redeemer, Emanuel, Lord, Mighty One, King, and Shepherd.
- Next consider what you desire or want from God today? If you have a specific request make it as short as possible and general as possible. Let general words represent your specific request.
- Put the two parts together. As you breathe in, say your name for God. As you breathe out, state your want or desire for today.

For example: Shepherd, guide me in your ways.
            or Jesus, grant me peace.

Following your breath, repeat your personal breath prayer for at least five minutes and then journal about the experience. Please note your chosen breath prayer.

____

____

____

____

Evening Prayer

Dear God, help me to be aware of how the Holy Spirit is addressing the blocks I have to a deeper relationship with you?

What emotion, attitude or issues did I become aware of today that are blocking my deeper relationship with God?

____

____

____

____

____

____

____

____

____

____

What opportunities did I miss today to deepen my relationship with God?

____

____

____

____

____

____

____

____

____

____

Dear God, thanks for today and for your guidance in this examen. I ask for your help and direction tomorrow so that I might follow your plan for my life more closely.

Morning Prayer

Colloquy with Jesus

To have a colloquy with Jesus means to have a casual intimate conversation. Set the scene by imagining Jesus sitting across from you, walking beside you, sitting at the foot of your bed, or simply being with you in an intimate setting. Now speak to Jesus as you would a friend, a lover, or a parent.

As you begin, remember that all conversations, when there is a back and forth, have moments of silence so you can hear what Jesus has to say to you. Also, remember the hallmarks of any intimate conversation are vulnerability and honesty. Be willing to share emotions including anger and disappointment as well as joy and thankfulness.

St. Ignatius, the saint who including the colloquy in his spiritual exercises, believed that imagination can be very helpful in our prayer life. So use your imagination to have a wonderful conversation with Jesus and allow your imagination to hear what Jesus says back.

____

____

____

____

____

____

Evening Prayer

Dear God, you say I am the light of the world. Help me to be aware of when my light shines and when it is dull.

When today did I live into my roll as the light of the world?

____

____

____

____

____

____

____

____

____

____

When today was my light dim or seemingly non-existent?

____

____

____

____

____

____

____

____

____

____

Dear God, thanks for today and for your guidance in this examen. I ask for your help and direction tomorrow so that I might follow your plan for my life more closely.

Morning Prayer

Centering Prayer

This is a simple prayer form in terms of instructions, but not in terms of practice. Before you begin:

- Decide how long you will be doing this prayer: 20 minutes is a good amount of time but start with 10 minutes if you have never done it before.
- Choose a sacred word that you will use to bring your attention back to sitting in silence and reaffirming your intention to surrender to the mystery of God.
- Find a comfortable place where you can sit.
- Remind yourself that just like your lungs breathe, your mind thinks, so try not to be upset by your distractions. Each time your mind wanders, simply bring your attention back to your sacred word.
- This prayer type fosters knowledge of God through experience.

Begin by asking Jesus to become real to you during this time of prayer and to help you let go of any specific outcomes for the time spent.

Take a few nice slow deep breaths and say your sacred word to yourself. Then begin to quietly sit and be open to being with God. Continue to say your word whenever any distracting thoughts come into your mind. Allow this word to bring you back to inner quietness.

When your set time is over, end by thanking God for this gift of silence and presence. Finally, journal for a few minutes.

____

____

Evening Prayer

Dear God, thank you for your love! Help me to review my day through the eyes of your grace and notice the ways you are working on me.

As I review my day, help me to notice moments that were great blessings and moment where I recognized your presence.

As I review my day, help me to recall moments where I didn't live into your opportunity, didn't recognize your presence or turned away from your call.

____

____

____

____

____

____

____

____

____

____

____

____

Dear God, thank you and guide me tomorrow along your holy path.

Morning Prayer

Guided Meditation

Take a few deep breaths and close your eyes and feel yourself relaxing. As you continue to breathe slowly and deeply, imagine that you are on a beach in a protected bay. Hear the gentle waves rolling in and the call of seagulls around you. Admire the beauty and how relaxed you feel as you see the waves rhythmically splash onto the shore wetting and smoothing the sand.

As you stand there fully relaxed, you are aware that someone holy is approaching. You see Jesus walking down the beach. . . Imagine him greeting you lovingly. . . He asked you if you want to enter the holy water? You walk into the water together. You feel the water gently swaying you back and forth.

Jesus looks into your eyes searching. He takes water into his hands and raises it over your head. You feel the water wetting your head and trickling down over your face as he says the words . . . "Do not let your heart be troubled." (John 14:1 NIV) You feel the troubles of your heart, your fears, loosening. . . You notice every place in your body where you have stored tension and worry letting it go. Your jaw relaxes, as do your neck and shoulders, and back. . . The tension flows out of your fingertips and toes into the surrounding water mixing in and disappearing.

Jesus again picks up a handful of water and pores it over the top of your head. You feel its warmth and healing energy, "Peace I leave with you; my peace I give you. (John 14:27 NIV) You feel his peace enter your body through the top of your head as the water again washes over your head and shoulders, neck and torso, legs and arms. This healing water cleans out every place in your body that use to be the home of worry. You feel the peace moving slowly down your body and further loosening every muscle and filling it with God's healing energy of peace.

Jesus scoops up a third handful of water. You are aware of the love that is in the water as he blesses it and again pours it over your head. He says, "When you live in love you live in Me." (paraphrase of John 17:23)

As this healing water flows over you, feel his love filling the places in your heart and body that were occupied by fear and worry. As more and more love flows in, the negative emotions flow out. They leave your head and heart, your shoulders and neck, your torso and legs. See and feel emotions flowing out and into the surrounding water where they disappear. . . As you stand there next to Jesus you are aware of every inch of your body being full of peace and love. You relish Jesus' gift to you today as you take a few minutes to thank him. When you are finished take write in your journal.

____

____

____

____

____

____

____

Evening Prayer

God, guide me in this honest examen today. Help me look at this day and everyday with appreciation and honesty.

For which moments today am I most thankful?

____

____

____

____

____

____

____

____

____

____

For which moments today am I least thankful?

Dear God, thanks for today and for your guidance in this examen. I ask for your help and direction tomorrow so that I might follow your plan for my life more closely.

Morning Prayer

A Subtractive Litany

My name for this type of prayer comes from the fact that it loses words with each iteration and it is a repetitive petition.

From Psalm 46:10 (NIV) Be still, and know that I am God.

Begin with the verse and then with each repetition lose the last word or phrase. Leave a minute of silence after each line to meditate on what stands out for you in each repetition.

Be still, and know that I am God.
Be still, and know that I am.
Be still, and know.
Be still.
Be.

Finish by spending a few minutes journaling about your experience.

____

____

____

____

____

Evening Prayer

God, help me to be aware of ways in which you delighted in me today and ways in which I was not as delightful.

When did I feel most delighted about my day or when did I feel God's delight in me as part of his creation?

____

____

____

____

____

____

____

____

____

____

When did I feel displeasure today or feel that perhaps God was displeased with my behavior.

____

____

____

____

____

____

____

____

____

____

____

Dear God, thanks for today and for your guidance in this examen. I ask for your help and direction tomorrow so that I might follow your plan for my life more closely.

Morning Prayer

Lectio Divina

Prepare for the Reading of the Word
Take three nice slow deep breaths and feel yourself relaxing.

Lectio
Read the below scripture and notice a word or phrase that catches your attention or tugs at your heart.

You are the light of the world. A town built on a hill cannot be hidden. Neither do people light a lamp and put it under a bowl. Instead they put it on its stand, and it gives light to everyone in the house. In the same way, let your light shine before others, that they may see your good deeds and glorify your Father in heaven. (Matthew 5:14-16 NIV)

Contemplatio (2 + min.)
Sit quietly, rest and prepare yourself to hear the word again.

Lectio
Read the scripture again and notice a word or phrase that captures your attention.

You are the light of the world. A town built on a hill cannot be hidden. Neither do people light a lamp and put it under a bowl. Instead they put it on its stand, and it gives light to everyone in the house. In the same way, let your light shine before others, that they may see your good deeds and glorify your Father in heaven.

Meditatio (5 + min.)
Spend some time meditating on your word or phrase. Allow God to speak to any situation you are going through using this scripture.

Oratio (5 + min.)
Speak your heart to God about your meditation and then journal.

Evening Prayer

Dear God, it seems an impossible task to love you with all my heart. Help me be aware of my breakthrough moments of love and my moment when fear and doubt dominated.

When did I love God and others today?

____

____

____

____

____

____

____

____

____

____

____

When were fear and doubt my major emotions?

____

____

____

____

____

____

____

____

____

____

Dear God, thanks for today and for your guidance in this examen. I ask for your help and direction tomorrow so that I might follow your plan for my life more closely.

Morning Prayer

Ignatian Contemplation

Begin by reading Mark 4:36-39 (NIV) listed below. Read it a couple of times so you are familiar with the story.

Leaving the crowd behind, they took him along, just as he was, in the boat. There were also other boats with him. A furious squall came up, and the waves broke over the boat, so that it was nearly swamped. Jesus was in the stern, sleeping on a cushion. The disciples woke him and said to him, "Teacher, don't you care if we drown?"
He got up, rebuked the wind and said to the waves, "Quiet! Be still!" Then the wind died down and it was completely calm.

Now allow yourself to enter the scene as any character.

Take a few deep breaths and relax. . . Get a sense of yourself being on the boat with Jesus. . . Notice the size of the boat and what it's made of. See the water around the boat. Is it rough or smooth? Now begin to observe a change in the weather . . . the clouds and wind are moving closer.

Feel the water splashing on you. . . See and feel the struggle with the boat. . . Now notice where Jesus is and how he is sleeping. . . Notice how it makes you feel. . . Do you want to wake him up right away or do you only do it in desperation? Now imagine yourself waking him up. . . What do you say to him? How does he look at you?

Now see Jesus calming the storm. . . How does it feel to have the waves die down and the wind ease?. . . How do you react to this miracle? How do you interact with Jesus after this miracle?

As you enter your time of journaling ask yourself: What stood out to you in prayer? What challenged you? Where did you sense God the most? What emotions were you aware of? What did you resist?

Date: _______________

Evening Prayer

Holy God, you love my humbleness and abhor pride. Help me to lovingly look at when I experienced each today?

When was I humble today?

____

____

____

____

____

____

____

____

____

____

When did pride get in the way of my work, accepting valid criticism, enjoying a conversation, or being happy for others?

Dear God, thanks for today and for your guidance in this examen. I ask for your help and direction tomorrow so that I might follow your plan for my life more closely.

Morning Prayer

Contemplative Reflection

Contemplative reflection is an unusual form of contemplative prayer that involves struggling with an issue or concept. It is sometimes described as wrestling with God.

When done on your own it involves choosing an article, quote, scripture, poem, or other religious text that is focused on a topic like love, faith, justice, or hope, for a few examples. Begin by asking God to guide your thoughts. Next, read the selected material and spend the chosen period of time contemplating the topic. For this morning's contemplative reflection read the below quote from Marjorie Thompson in *Soul Feast:*

In Christ we are reshaped according to the pattern we were created to bear. This reshaping is the basic meaning of spiritual formation in the Christian tradition. The term formation lies at the heart of words like conformation, reformation, and transformation. It invites us to consider: What or whose form are we seeking? What, in our personal or corporate lives, needs to be reformed?

Meditate or wrestle with the topic for 10 minutes or more. End by journaling about the experience.

____

____

____

____

Evening Prayer

God, help me be aware of the times today that I noticed and appreciated your majesty and Also help me to remember when I got stuck in complaining.

When today was I in awe of the world God created?

____

____

____

____

____

____

____

____

____

____

____

____

____

____

____

____

____

____

____

____

____

Dear God, thanks for today and for your guidance in this examen. I ask for your help and direction tomorrow so that I might follow your plan for my life more closely.

Morning Prayer

A Personal Lectio

Listen to Your Week

As you relax, take a couple of minutes to review the moments of your week. Allow each event and interaction to gentle move into and out of your awareness. As you continue to breath deeply, begin to focus on one occasion that seems to pull your attention and have more emotional energy.

Listen to the Moment

Now sit with this occasion or event for a couple of minutes and recreate the physical event as much as possible. Remember the sounds, colors, smells, and how it progressed.

Then remember your emotions during this event. When were your emotions the strongest? How did they feel in your body? Especially notice any change in your emotions. Spend a couple of minutes contemplating this event.

Listen to God

Now allow yourself to let go of this moment. Let go of the feelings you experienced during the event and allow your mind to go as blank as possible as you release everything about this moment to God. With a blank mind, invite God to give you an image, a phrase, a song, a thought or a scripture that relates to this moment. Be open to whatever comes to mind without having to understand how it relates to your moment. Trust and accept it gratefully.

Offering

Now in your mind, take the incident, and the image or phrase given by God, and place them both on an offering plate. Offer this plate with its images up to God. Give God all that was done and all that wasn't, all you regrets and all you are thankful for. Give God all your emotions. Give it all back to God as you open yourself to any gifts God wants to give you through this prayer.

Thanksgiving
End with a prayer of thanksgiving for any grace, any gifts, or any struggles that you received during this prayer time. Finish with a few minutes of journal writing.

Adapted from A Personal Lectio Process from Heartpath DFW

Evening Prayer

Holy God, help me to notice the moments in my day that were filled with compassion and also those moment when compassion was far from my heart.

When today was I compassionate to both others and myself?

____

____

____

____

____

____

____

____

____

____

When today was I impatient and uncaring both to other people's diffi-culties and my own?

____

____

____

____

____

____

____

____

____

____

Dear God, thanks for today and for your guidance in this examen. I ask for your help and direction tomorrow so that I might follow your plan for my life more closely.

Morning Prayer

A Personal Breath Prayer

Design your own personal breath prayer with these simple steps. This prayer may be prayed out loud or to yourself.

- Start with your favorite name for God. You can look to scriptures for these names but here are a few suggestions to get you started: Jesus, Creator, Father, God, Counselor, Prince of Peace, Savior, Redeemer, Emanuel, Lord, Mighty One, King, and Shepherd.
- Next consider what you desire or want from God today? If you have a specific request make it as short as possible and general as possible. Let general words represent your specific request.
- Put the two parts together. As you breathe in, say your name for God. As you breathe out, state your want or desire for today.

For example: Shepherd, guide me in your ways.
or Jesus, grant me peace.

Following your breath repeat for at least five minutes and then journal about the experience. Please note your chosen prayer.

____

____

____

____

Evening Prayer

Dear God, I know you tell me that I should take refuge in you, but I often don't. Help me to be honest about the times that I take refuge in other things and people instead of running to you.

When today did I take refuge in God?

____

____

____

____

____

____

____

____

____

____

____

____

____

____

____

____

____

____

____

____

Dear God, thanks for today and for your guidance in this examen. I ask for your help and direction tomorrow so that I might follow your plan for my life more closely.

Morning Prayer

Colloquy with Jesus

To have a colloquy with Jesus means to have a casual intimate conversation. Set the scene by imagining Jesus sitting across from you, walking beside you, sitting at the foot of your bed, or simply being with you in an intimate setting. Now speak to Jesus as you would a friend, a lover, or a parent.

As you begin, remember that all conversations, when there is a back and forth, have moments of silence so you can hear what Jesus has to say to you. Also, remember the hallmarks of any intimate conversation are vulnerability and honesty. Be willing to share emotions including anger and disappointment as well as joy and thankfulness.

St. Ignatius, the saint who including the colloquy in his spiritual exercises, believed that imagination can be very helpful in our prayer life. So use your imagination to have a wonderful conversation with Jesus and allow your imagination to hear what Jesus says back.

____

____

____

____

____

____

Evening Prayer

Dear God, sometimes during the day I draw closer to you and sometimes I find I just want to do my day my way. Help me to be aware of these moments and their affects on both my spirit and my relationships.

When did I draw closer to God today?

____

____

____

____

____

____

____

____

____

____

What moments today did I move away from God in my thoughts and actions?

____

____

____

____

____

____

____

____

____

____

Dear God, thanks for today and for your guidance in this examen. I ask for your help and direction tomorrow so that I might follow your plan for my life more closely.

Morning Prayer

Centering Prayer

This is a simple prayer form in terms of instructions, but not in terms of practice. Before you begin:

- Decide how long you will be doing this prayer: 20 minutes is a good amount of time but start with 10 minutes if you have never done it before.
- Choose a sacred word that you will use to bring your attention back to sitting in silence and reaffirming your intention to surrender to the mystery of God.
- Find a comfortable place where you can sit.
- Remind yourself that just like your lungs breathe, your mind thinks, so try not to be upset by your distractions. Each time your mind wanders, simply bring your attention back to your sacred word.
- This prayer type fosters knowledge of God through experience.

Begin by asking Jesus to become real to you during this time of prayer and to help you let go of any specific outcomes for the time spent.

Take a few nice slow deep breaths and say your sacred word to yourself. Then begin to quietly sit and be open to being with God. Continue to say your word whenever any distracting thoughts come into your mind. Allow this word to bring you back to inner quietness.

When your set time is over, end by thanking God for this gift of silence and presence. Finally, journal for a few minutes.

Evening Prayer

Dear God, there are people, that in my opinion, have wronged me and my loved ones. Blessing them, forgiving them, is your will but I admit it is difficult to even want their lives to turn out well. Help me to let go of my grievances today and every day.

When today did I work on blessing my enemies or at least not wishing them harm? When did I want good for people who seem to not want good for me?

Who did I have trouble forgiving today? What "wrong" did I keep wanting to bring up? When I prayed who was it hard to pray for?

Dear God, thanks for today and for your guidance in this examen. I ask for your help and direction tomorrow so that I might follow your plan for my life more closely.

Morning Prayer

Guided Meditation

The following is a guided meditation based on Acts 16: 25-26: About midnight Paul and Silas were praying and singing hymns to God, and the other prisoners were listening to them. Suddenly there was such a violent earthquake that the foundations of the prison were shaken. At once all the prison doors flew open, and everyone's chains came loose.

Read over the following meditation slowly, resting each time there are ellipsis. Refer back to this page when necessary. You can also record this meditation on your phone.

Take a few deep breaths and close your eyes and feel yourself relaxing. As you continue to breathe slowly and deeply, imagine yourself in a prison. . . There are bars all around you. Each bar is labeled pertaining to the emotion or trouble that is keeping you locked up in some way. . . They could be labeled "fear," "anxiety," "hatred," or any emotion. Spend a few moments and imagine those bars around you and how they are stopping you from living the life God wants you to live. Know what it is like to live surrounded by these bars. . .

Now feel God's presence around you. . . The earth beneath you begins shaking . . . It is a shake that comes from great power. . . You watch as all the bars surrounding you dissolve and fall.

Seeing the rods that once surround you now on the ground, you step over them and out into the open. Become aware that you have witnessed God's great power. . . When you were behind the bars they seemed solid and strong; now you see they were not. Relish what it is like to live free. . .

End this time by thanking God for this experience and then journal below.

Evening Prayer

God, help me to be aware of ways in which you bring joy or try to bring joy into my life.

When did I feel God's joy today?

When did I feel God trying to change my focus but I was unable or unwilling to change?

____

____

____

____

____

____

____

____

____

____

Dear God, thanks for today and for your guidance in this examen. I ask for your help and direction tomorrow so that I might follow your plan for my life more closely.

Morning Prayer

Lectio Divina

Prepare for the Reading of the Word
Take three nice slow deep breaths and feel yourself relaxing.

Lectio
Read the below scripture and notice a word or phrase that catches your attention or tugs at your heart.

I will sprinkle clean water on you, and you will be clean; I will cleanse you from all your impurities and from all your idols. I will give you a new heart and put a new spirit in you; I will remove from you your heart of stone and give you a heart of flesh. And I will put my Spirit in you and move you to follow my decrees and be careful to keep my laws. (Ezekiel 36:25-27 NIV)

Contemplatio (2 + min.)
Sit quietly, rest and prepare yourself to hear the word again.

Lectio
Read the scripture again and notice a word or phrase that captures your attention.

I will sprinkle clean water on you, and you will be clean; I will cleanse you from all your impurities and from all your idols. I will give you a new heart and put a new spirit in you; I will remove from you your heart of stone and give you a heart of flesh. And I will put my Spirit in you and move you to follow my decrees and be careful to keep my laws.

Meditatio (5 + min.)
Spend some time meditating on your word or phrase. Allow God to speak to any situation you are going through using this scripture.

Oratio (5 + min.)

Speak your heart to God about this meditation and journal below.

Evening Prayer

God, as I review my day, help me to be aware of moments when you were clearly working both on me and in my life and when I was attempting to run the other way.

When did it seem that God was most involved with me today?

____

____

____

____

____

____

____

____

____

____

When today was I totally oblivious to God working in my life?

____

____

____

____

____

____

____

____

____

____

____

Dear God, thanks for today and for your guidance in this examen. I ask for your help and direction tomorrow so that I might follow your plan for my life more closely.

Works Sited for Contemplative Reflections

May, Gerald G. M.D. *Addiction and Grace,* Harper Collins, 1991

Rohr, Richard *Everything Belongs,* The Crossroad Publishing Company, 1999

Thompson, Marjorie *Soul Feast,* Westminster John Knox Press, 1995.

As you reach the end of this journal take some time to look back and see where God has been in your days, weeks, and month. Make notes and process your experience on the next few pages. Consider some of the following questions:

- Is there some issue or needed growth that God seems to be continually pointing out to you in your prayer time?
- How is God working on you?
- In what ways are you resisting this work?
- In what ways are you embracing this work?
- Are you drawn to variety in prayer? How can you support that need?
- Is there any practice you resisted doing? What is that resistance about?
- Which contemplative practice bears the most fruit for you?
- Which practices help you to sense and experience God the most?
- Which practice or practices will you continue?

Other Books by the Author

This *Examen Journal* will help you establish the powerful daily practice of noticing when you are moving away from God and when you are moving towards him. This spiritual tool combines daily practice of The Examen with room to journal.

Walking with God. Quickly jot down your God moments one line at a time. This formatted journal is the perfect way to record all your God appointments: answered prayers, moments when God speaks to your heart, amazing miracle, and God's guidance. This journal is especially suited for those who want to remember but don't have the time for longer entries or enjoy writing.

Faith Marker Journey: A Sacred Journey to Guide you into a Deeper Relationship with Christ. This powerful book both explains how to mark you faith and all the many benefits of this ancient spiritual practice.

If I Only Had… Wrapping Yourself in God's Truth During Storms of Insecurity is an award winning answer–focused book for women who've searched for security in looks, friends, family, money, and men, and have come up empty–handed.

Pearls of Promise: A Devotional Designed to Reassure You of God's Love is a *Chicken Soup for the Soul* type book designed to comfort and encourage you.